SQUADRONS!

No. 53

THE HAWKER
HURRICANE MK I & II
- THE EAGLE SQUADRONS -

PHIL H. LISTEMANN

ISBN: 979-1096490-90-5

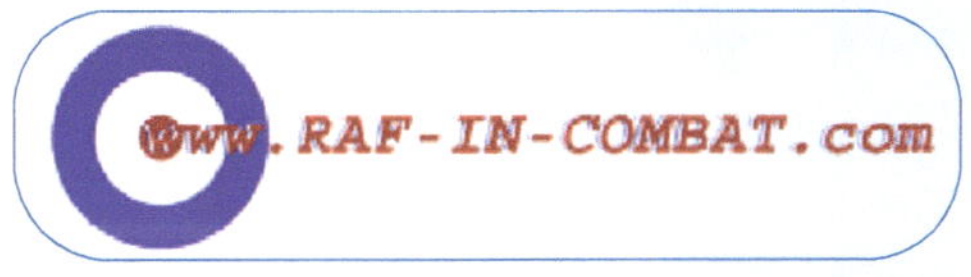

Colour profiles: Gaetan Marie/Bravo Bravo Aviation

GLOSSARY OF TERMS

PERSONEL :

(AUS)/RAF: Australian serving in the RAF
(BEL)/RAF: Belgian serving in the RAF
(CAN)/RAF: Canadian serving in the RAF
(CZ)/RAF: Czechoslovak serving in the RAF
(NFL)/RAF: Newfoundlander serving in the RAF
(NL)/RAF: Dutch serving in the RAF
(NZ)/RAF: New Zealander serving in the RAF
(POL)/RAF: Pole serving in the RAF
(RHO)/RAF: Rhodesian serving in the RAF
(SA)/RAF: South African serving in the RAF
(US)/RAF - RCAF : American serving in the RAF or RCAF

RANKS

G/C : Group Captain
W/C : Wing Commander
S/L : Squadron Leader
F/L : Flight Lieutenant
F/O : Flying Officer
P/O : Pilot Officer
W/O : Warrant Officer
F/Sgt : Flight Sergeant
Sgt : Sergeant
Cpl : Corporal
LAC : Leading Aircraftman

OTHER

ATA: Air Transport Auxiliary
CO : Commander
DFC : Distinguished Flying Cross
DFM : Distinguished Flying Medal
DSO : Distinguished Service Order
Eva. : Evaded
ORB : Operational Record Book
OTU : Operational Training Unit
PoW : Prisoner of War
PAF: Polish Air Force
RAF : Royal Air Force
RAAF : Royal Australian Air Force
RCAF : Royal Canadian Air Force
RNZAF : Royal New Zealand Air Force
SAAF : South African Air Force
s/d: Shot down
Sqn : Squadron
† : Killed

CODE-NAMES - OFFENSIVE OPERATIONS - FIGHTER COMMAND

CIRCUS:

Bombers heavily escorted by fighters, the purpose being to bring enemy fighters into combat.

RAMROD:

Bombers escorted by fighters, the primary aim being to destroy a target.

RANGER:

Large formation freelance intrusion over enemy territory with aim of wearing down enemy fighters.

RHUBARB:

Freelance fighter sortie against targets of opportunity.

ROADSTEAD:

Dive bombing and low level attacks on enemy ships at sea or in harbour

RODEO:

A fighter sweep without bombers.

SWEEP:

An offensive flight by fighters designed to draw up and clear the enemy from the sky.

The Hawker Hurricane

The Hawker Hurricane was the first of the modern fighter types to begin re-equipping the RAF in the 1930s. When introduced in 1937, the RAF only had biplane fighters, descendants of the Great War designs, on hand. The story of the Hurricane began in October 1933 and the prototype, K5083, was ordered on 21 February 1935. The maiden flight occurred on the following 6 November. As the RAF was now undergoing a massive expansion, the Hurricane, which performed well during its trials, was soon ordered in large numbers. In June 1936, the first order was placed for 600 aircraft. In November 1938, just after the Munich Crisis, another order was placed for 1000. When war broke out almost 500 Hurricanes had been delivered to Fighter Command and that number had reached 2300 one year later. The Hurricane remained the backbone of the RAF's fighter force at least until 1942 in Europe, 1943 in the Mediterranean and the Middle East, and 1944 in the Far East, when more modern types were introduced or became more plentiful. It remained in frontline inventory in the Middle and Far East until the very last days of the war. Indeed, while the Hurricane as a pure fighter was easily obsolete by that time, it proved to be a fine fighter-bomber. The concept was introduced in late 1941, initially with bombs, but the Hurricane would also be successfully equipped with rockets and 40mm cannons. The Hurricane's main fault, however, was that, unlike the Spitfire, no major improvements or modifications could be made to the airframe and that condemned the type from the beginning.

The Hurricane was involved in most of the first combats against the Luftwaffe over France and then over Britain. The basic model was continually improved and the Mk.II appeared in 1941 with an improved Rolls-Royce Merlin, the III, rated at 1030 hp, giving way to the Merlin XX of 1460 hp. The armament was also improved, with the increasing number of 0.303-in machine-guns in the wings, eight and then twelve, being replaced by four 20mm cannons.

Being an impressive aircraft at the end of the thirties, the Hurricane attracted interest from foreign countries and the Dominions. Before the war, and just after the war broke out, the Hurricane was exported to Belgium, Yugoslavia, Rumania, Finland and Turkey. South Africa was also interested and purchased some aircraft to modernise its fighter force. Canada did the same.

Recruiting American Pilots

From the very beginning of the war in Europe, Americans, at all levels, took an interest in the conflict realising that, sooner or later, they would be involved. Creating a fighter squadron comprising American volunteers quickly took root in certain minds, including Charles Sweeny's, an ex-serviceman of the French Foreign Legion during the Great War. He had been inspired by the exploits of the famous American-manned Lafayette squadron, and the status it held, all of which had been portrayed by the media of the time. He established a network, allowing interested Americans to cross the Atlantic to support France, although French enthusiasm on this occasion was not so positive. Compounding Sweeny's problems was a Congress Neutrality Act, voted in 1935 and revised and reinforced many times thereafter, making the recruiting of American volunteers for fighting in foreign countries very difficult

Side view of the prototype Hurricane K5083. The Hurricane had excellent performance for the time, but by 1941 it had already reached its limits. It would continue to serve with success as a fighter-bomber until the end of the war.

The man who started it all, Colonel Sweeny, right, in RAF uniform. He served with the French Foreign Legion in early W.W.I and soon found himself in charge of its small American unit. In 1915 he was commissioned in the Legion, the first American to be so promoted. He was wounded the same year and was also the first American to be awarded the Legion of Honour. When the USA entered the war, he joined the US Army and ended the war as a lieutenant-colonel. He continued his career as a soldier of fortune post- war and, logically, when France was at war once more in 1939, he wished to help build a new Lafayette *escadrille*. France collapsed before the project came to fruition, but the RAF would inherit the project.

indeed. The US authorities closely monitored activity of this nature and would not facilitate any enlistment. Volunteers or, for that matter, anyone suspected of being one, would be detained at the Canadian border. This situation remained right up until the fall of France in June 1940. As a result, volunteers arrived too late and the French, overwhelmed by their own situation, had little to offer them. Consequently, the vast majority disappeared amid the upheaval, either killed or made prisoners, while others returned to the USA by their own means. Only five of the original volunteers are known to have arrived in Great Britain.

Thereafter the situation changed and American authorities became more accommodating. At the same time the number of volunteers increased, since many were aware that the USA was preparing to enter the war. The Knight Committee, named for its founder, was set up and this organisation would be responsible for the bulk of American recruitment from the spring of 1940. In August 1941 this committee became the Canadian Aviation Bureau before it was disbanded in late 1942. Some 250 American pilots would serve with three American fighter units - the Eagle Squadrons - formed within the RAF between 1940 and 1942. These men, though, were only a fraction of the hundreds who passed through the committee to enrol in the RAF, or the RCAF, and fight under the RAF umbrella in Europe, the Middle East and the Far East. Their motives were varied, but the majority simply sought adventure. Their aspirations were to become pilots, but many had been refused entry into their own country's air arms on educational, competency or medical grounds (or a combination of those). Both the RCAF and the RAF (Royal Air Force Volunteer Reserve - RAFVR) provided viable alternatives and the prospect of flying a Spitfire, by then the best Allied fighter, only strengthened their desire to join up. The American pilots, in particular those that served with the Eagle Squadrons, were to benefit from certain privileges. Most were not required to pledge allegiance to the King upon their engagement and thus were able to maintain their American citizenship. Additionally, it was understood that, those passed by the Knight Committee would be commissioned at the end of their training, as opposed to the majority of those who joined the RCAF and graduated as Non-Commissioned Officers. This disparity was to create problems when the integration of these pilots into the USAAF took place.

Victories - confirmed or probable claims: 12.5

Number of sorties: *ca.* 2,325

First operational sortie:
05.02.41
Last operational sortie:
19.08.41

Total aircraft written-off: 10

Aircraft lost on operations: 7
Aircraft lost in accidents: 3

Squadron code letters:
XR

COMMANDING OFFICERS

S/L Walter M. CHURCHILL	AAF No. 90241	AAF	...	23.01.41
S/L William E.G. TAYLOR	RAF No. 86597	(US)/RAF	23.01.41	05.06.41
S/L Henry de C.A. WOODHOUSE	RAF No. 34189	RAF	05.06.41	13.08.41
S/L Ernest R. BITMEAD	RAF No. 34139	RAF	13.08.41	...

SQUADRON USAGE

Activated on 27 March 1917, No. 71 Squadron at first mainly comprised Australian personnel serving with the Royal Flying Corps. It left for France in December with its Sopwith Camels. The unit was finally renamed No. 4 Squadron, Australian Flying Corps, on 19 January 1918. Number 71 Squadron was not 're-born' until the Second World War when American volunteers in the RAF were brought together as a unit.

While the USA did not immediately get involved in both conflicts, resourceful Americans, seeking adventure, wanting to fight against tyranny or anticipating the eventual entry of their country into the war, signed up to fight. During the First World War, an American-manned fighter squadron, the *Escadrille Lafayette*, had been activated in France to fly with the *Aéronautique Militaire*. It was named after a French hero of the American War of Independence.

As early as the beginning of WW2, American volunteers rushed toward the recruiting offices to fight in Europe. Canada was the main entry because of its proximity, but some tried their chances via other channels to join French units. While some would set foot on the Continent, none would be trained by the French; many ended up in Great Britain. The first trained American volunteers were transferred to different units of the RAF; a few even participated in the Battle of Britain, some paying with their lives. Faced with an increased influx of American volunteers, grouping them together as a fighter unit was envisaged. The idea was accepted as early as 2 July 1940. This was a time when the RAF activated many units comprising volunteers from the occupied European countries. It was important for Britain to show the rest of the world they were not the only ones willing to fight. Three fighter units, principally comprising American citizens, would be created and came to be

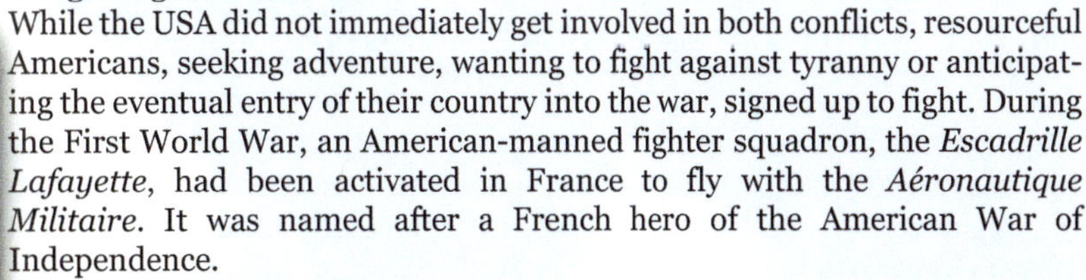

William EG Taylor was a former USN and USMC pilot who rose to the rank of captain before enlisting in the Fleet Air Arm in 1939; he fought in Norway in 1940. Later, he transferred to the RAF and became the first American CO of an Eagle squadron. He eventually ended the war as a USN captain.

Twelve of the first American pilots to serve with the squadron, in late April 1941. Left to right:
Charles E. Bateman from Massachusetts, William H. Nichols from California (PoW 07.09.41), Stanley M. Kolendorski from New Jersey (†17.05.41), William EG Taylor (CO) from Kansas, Andrew B. Mamedoff from Connecticut (†08.10.41 with 133 Sqn), Eugene Q. Tobin from Utah (†07.09.41), Newton Anderson from Louisiana (†29.06.42 as CO of 222 Sqn, the first American to lead an all-British fighter squadron), Luke E. Allen from Colorado, Ken S. Taylor from Manitoba, Canada (†08.08.41), Victor R. Bono born in Norway, Gregory A. Daymond from Montana, and Sam A. Mauriello from New York. All the Eagle pilots who passed through the Knight Committee received a commission upfront. All of the surviving pilots transferred to the USAAF, but Allen resigned his RAF commission later that spring, apparently for personal reasons. Bono, more obscurely, was dismissed from RAF service in March 1942. Note the first name 'Maud' painted under the cockpit.

known as the Eagle Squadrons. Only the pilots who served with one or more of the three fighter units, between 1940 and 1942, could be designated as Eagles; Americans serving with other units of the RAF or RCAF could not. It was the same for the pilots coming from the American fighter schools, who would later form the 4th Fighter Group (FG), and who in fact had nothing to do with the RAF or the RCAF, even though this unit was the direct descendant of the three Eagle Squadrons. To distinguish themselves from Americans in the RAF and RCAF who simply wore a 'USA' shoulder flash, the Eagle pilots had a special badge made.

After the Battle of Britain, 71 Squadron reformed at Church Fenton. The three Eagle Squadrons were to receive a number in the RAF's regular sequence, not what was normally reserved for squadrons consisting of mainly non-British pilots (the 300 series, for example) as the ground personnel would be mostly British and would remain so during the units' period of existence. From the first day of 71 Squadron's service, three pilots, already serving elsewhere with operational units, were transferred in. They were Pilot Officers E. Tobin, AB Mamedoff and V. Keough. Command of the squadron was given to a British pilot, S/L W.M. Churchill, who assumed the role on 29 September, while the flight commander positions were filled a month later, again by British pilots (Flight Lieutenants G.A. Brown and R.C. Wilkinson). For the Americans, this situation was not at first looked upon favourably as they wanted a 100% American unit under the command of the RAF, nothing less. The formation of 71 was highly publicised by the British who needed to show that Americans were already fighting at their side. For these purposes, no British pilots were present in the photographs released to the media. It was a big disappointment, especially for William Taylor, an ex-USN pilot, who had expected to command the squadron but instead became Churchill's deputy. The reality for the RAF, however, having already commissioned several similar squadrons, was that the 'newcomers' needed to gain experience, not just in action against the Luftwaffe, but in the way the RAF did things. It, therefore, had been agreed that leadership roles would be filled by Americans once this requisite experience had been acquired. Meanwhile, the pilots slowly arrived but training was not homogenous (71 Squadron comprised several relatively experienced flyers as already mentioned), as the vast majority of assigned pilots were fresh from schools and needed to complete their training. The squadron eventually attained its normal quota of pilots towards the end of November. Meanwhile, on 8 October 1940, the British officially announced the existence of No. 71 (Eagle) Squadron. Regarding the aircraft, the first arrived

This page and next. Like many squadrons, 71 began working up on war-weary Hurricane Mk.Is. By the spring of 1941, these were replaced by brand-new Hurricane Mk.IIs, which had better performance. The Hurricanes are wearing post-Battle of Britain camouflage and markings, most of the time masking the serials. However, 'XR-J' above was V7608 and (next page) 'XR-F' was V7319.

Among the founding members of the squadron were three Battle of Britain veterans: Eugene Q. Tobin from Utah, Vernon C. Keough from New Jersey, and Andrew B. Mamedoff from Connecticut. All had previously flown with 609 Sqn and were posted together to the newly formed Eagle squadron. The latter is proudly displaying the badge adopted by all the American pilots posted to the Eagle squadrons. All three were killed during 1941, Tobin and Keough with 71 Sqn and Mamedoff with 133 Sqn.

on 24 October; they were three Brewster Buffaloes, recovered from a Belgian contract. The choice of this small fighter was odd, but may have been an attempt to get the Americans flying with something 'familiar'. The Brewsters were quickly judged unfit for combat by S/L Churchill himself who opposed the sending of additional machines. One of the aircraft was damaged by P/O Leckrone on 28 October, when he overturned during landing. At the same time, Churchill managed to obtain a quick replacement and, on 7 November, 71 took charge of its first nine Hurricane Mk.Is. They were far from new aircraft and the majority had seen combat during the preceding weeks so were a bit weary. They were certainly better than the Buffaloes, though, which left the squadron on 10 November. To complete its training, the unit left for Kirton in Lindsey, a base that would be used until April 1941. Despite unfavourable weather, training continued to bring the squadron up to an operational standard. This would not be without incident, however, as after the engine failure suffered by P/O V. Keough on the first day of the 1941, necessitating an emergency landing near the station, Pilot Officers P. Leckrone and E. Orbison collided in mid-air five days later. While Orbison manage to return to Kirton in Lindsey, Leckrone was left with no option but to abandon his out-of-control Hurricane. For unknown reasons, he was unable to do so and was killed in the subsequent crash. Leckrone was one of the seven American pilots to have participated in the Battle of Britain and his experience was of great value to the unit at this early stage. At the end of the month, Churchill had to leave for medical reasons and was temporarily replaced by S/L W. Taylor. During his command, Taylor instilled in his pilots an impeccable discipline which, while not always appreciated, would be helpful in the following weeks. The squadron was finally declared operational at the end of January 1941.

On 5 February, 71 Squadron carried out its first sortie, a patrol by Pilot Officers C.G. Peterson and L. Allen between 13.18 and 14.20. Local patrols comprised all of the squadron's early operational sorties, easing the unit in as it were. At the time, while the squadron had been declared operational, not all its pilots were regarded similarly. Early in the month one, P/O K.F. Kennerly, was even sent back to the USA due to his unsuitability. Operational flying may have started quietly, but two pilots were killed within a few weeks. Pilot Officer Orbison, having survived the mid-air collision with the now late Leckrone, ran out of luck on the 9th when he lost control of his aircraft during a patrol. Six days later, P/O V.C. Keough, another Battle of Britain veteran (No. 609 Squadron), was seen to crash into the water at great speed during a sortie over the North Sea. It was later discovered he had apparently not turned his

The first American pilot to be killed in action against the Luftwaffe was P/O 'Mike' Kolendorski. From New Jersey, he was proud of his Polish roots and displayed the Polish Air Force national markings on his flying suit. He's seen here jumping into a Hurricane for the camera. Note the aircraft is wearing the Eagle squadron badge painted under the exhaust pipes; this was not a very common practice.

oxygen on properly and lost consciousness as a result. Fifty-two sorties were carried out in February, followed by ninety more in March, but still combat claims eluded the Americans. The disappointing results were such that sending the pilots home, if things didn't improve in the weeks to come, was considered an option. In the hope of making things more favourable, 71 Squadron was transferred to the south-east of England on 9 April, coming under the command of No. 11 Group at Martlesham Heath, where encounters with the Luftwaffe were more likely. This change seemed to bear fruit as early as 13 April when the first German aircraft was encountered; the Ju88 escaped into cloud. The number of sorties increased to 190 in April, still without results. Worse, another loss was suffered when P/O J.L. McGinnis was killed on take-off for a patrol on 26 April. During the last days of April, 71 began to exchange its ageing Hurricane Mk.Is for Mk.IIs; the first sorties on the new aircraft were carried out on the 20th. By the end of April, all of the old machines were gone. May was the month of major changes. On the 9th, B Flight saw a change of command as P/O C.G. Peterson, an American, took over. A few days later, 71 finally opened its score. On the 15th, ten Hurricanes scrambled from Martlesham Heath at 20.30. They were soon ordered to patrol Canterbury at 20,000 feet. When over the city, they were vectored 150° for eight minutes and then told to orbit. They were flying over Calais in sections of two at 22,000 feet when Bf109s were spotted 2,000 feet below. Red Section, led by F/L G.A. Brown, dived after the enemy aircraft but could not catch up, rejoining the rest of the squadron at 21,000 feet. Yellow Section, led by P/O J.K .Alexander, which had followed Red Section down, continued the chase and Alexander was able to fire a two-second burst from 500 yards astern at a Bf109 without effect; the pursuit, however, had put Yellow Section in a very bad position as they were soon attacked by other Bf109s. Fortunately, the rest of the squadron joined them and a furious dogfight ensued. Alexander again managed to fire a long burst at another Bf109 from astern, this time closing to 150 yards. He saw his fire enter the Bf109 which climbed steeply for 500 feet, pouring black smoke, and suddenly nosed over into an uncontrolled spin towards the sea from 10,000 feet. Alexander did not see the Bf109 crash as he was obliged to assist his wingman, P/O J. Flynn, who had been attacked and badly damaged; the offending Bf109 had, in the meantime, abandoned the attack when he saw the English coast, but Flynn needed assistance to make his way back so was escorted by Alexander to Manston where he crash landed. Pilot Officer Alexander went on to claim a Bf109 probably destroyed. The Germans got their revenge two days later by shooting down P/O S. Kolendorski, when, while patrolling with nine others, he decided to chase a Bf109 and broke formation without orders, possibly falling into a trap. He was the first Eagle pilot to be killed in action. Despite this loss, May was seen as a positive; the Americans were happy to be in the thick of the action and flew more than 450 sorties for the month.
In June, Taylor was replaced by a British pilot, S/L Woodhouse, but, despite close to 600 sorties being flown, the month was otherwise uneventful. On the 23rd, 71 moved to North Weald. On 2 July, the squadron flew its first offensive mission by escorting

Hurricane Mk.IIs of 71 Sqn at dispersal at Martlesham Heath during the summer of 1941. Some aircraft appear ready for an immediate take-off, as seen by the parachutes on the stabilisers.

Blenheims to Lille where they were tasked to bomb a power station. The formation was intercepted by 24 Bf109s after reaching the town and in the ensuing melee three were claimed as destroyed (the CO, and Pilot Officers W.R. Dunn and G.A. Daymond), one probably destroyed (P/O R.L. Mannix) and one damaged (P/O V.R. Bono). Pilot Officer W.I. Hall, however, was lost to the Bf109s. He was seen to drop out of the fight with smoke pouring from his aircraft but was later reported as a PoW. Two days later, P/O K.S. Taylor added a Bf109, damaged near Bethune, to 71's scoreboard and, on the 6th, near Lille, Daymond added another Bf109 confirmed, while F/L C.G .Peterson claimed a Bf109 probably destroyed and Dunn shared one with a Polish pilot from No. 306 Squadron. The squadron continued its success two weeks later when Bono claimed a Bf109 probably destroyed west of Lille on the 19th and Dunn claimed another destroyed over the same place two days later. At the end of July, P/O A.B. Mamedoff became A Flight CO opposite F/L R.C. Wilkinson; now 71 had two American flight commanders. In August, the first Eagle Squadron continued its run of success. On the 3rd, while on a convoy patrol off Orfordness, Daymond caught a marauding Do17. Closing in, he opened fire from about 250 yards with a three-second burst; the rear gunner returned fire but ceased after the second burst fired by Daymond who continued his attack, firing his remaining ammunition. The Dornier hit the water and bounced off, before settling and sinking immediately. Sadly, two days later, P/O W.R. Driver was killed heading out for a sweep; he was seen in a dive, for unknown reasons, a mile north of Middle Waltham. The winds of change had begun to blow when the first Spitfire Mk.IIs arrived (see *SQUADRONS! 38*). The Hurricanes continued to be used, however, and the last claims were made on 19 August, coinciding with the last sorties performed on the type. While providing an escort to Blenheims for *Circus* 82, 71 was intercepted by Bf109s off Gravelines. Two claims were made: P/O M.W. Fessler for one Bf109 probably destroyed, while another was damaged by P/O H.S. Fenlaw. It wasn't a one-sided encounter, though, as P/O V.W. Olson was apparently hit by flak. Rather than bale out over France to become a prisoner, Olson elected to take his chances and nurse his stricken aircraft out over the North Sea where he baled out. Although his parachute was seen to open properly, he was never found. His body was eventually recovered on the Dutch coast. The next day, the squadron took off in the Spitfire Mk.IIs, closing the Hurricane era which had seen over 2,325 sorties flown (all but 320 on the Mk.IIs).

'Gus' Daymond was celebrated as being the first American ace of WW2, even though, technically speaking, it was 'Bill' Dunn. At twenty years old, he was one of the youngest pilots in the unit when he joined 71. He would eventually become one of the first American DFC recipients and, in September 1942, he assumed command of 71 just before its transfer to the USAAF as the 334th Fighter Squadron (he would lead that unit until March 1943). That was his last operational assignment as he served the remainder of the war as a test pilot.

Date	Pilot	SN	Origin	Type	Serial	Code	Nb	Cat.
15.05.41	P/O John K. **Alexander**	RAF No. 86618	(US)/RAF	Bf109	**Z2756**		1.0	P
02.07.41	S/L Henry de C.A. **Woodhouse**	RAF No. 34189	RAF	Bf109	**Z3345**	XR-H	1.0	C
	P/O William R. **Dunn**	RAF No. 60510	(US)/RAF	Bf109	**Z3781**	XR-A	1.0	C
	P/O Robert L. **Mannix**	RAF No. 64864	(US)/RAF	Bf109	**Z3335**	XR-F	1.0	P
	P/O Gregory A. **Daymond**	RAF No. 84657	(US)/RAF	Bf109	**Z3185**		1.0	C
06.07.41	P/O Gregory A. **Daymond**	RAF No. 84657	(US)/RAF	Bf109	**Z3829**		1.0	C
	F/L Chesley G. **Peterson**	RAF No. 83706	(US)/RAF	Bf109	**Z3170**		1.0	P
	P/O William R. **Dunn**	RAF No. 60510	(US)/RAF	Bf109	**Z3267**		0.5	P
	Shared with P/O L. Jaugsch of No.306 (Polish) Sqn.							
19.07.41	P/O Victor R. **Bono**	RAF No. 85220	(US)/RAF	Bf109	**Z3266**		1.0	P
21.07.41	P/O William R. **Dunn**	RAF No. 60510	(US)/RAF	Bf109	**Z3781**	XR-A	1.0	C
02.08.41	P/O Gregory A. **Daymond**	RAF No. 84657	(US)/RAF	Do17	**Z3182**		1.0	C
09.08.41	P/O William R. **Dunn**	RAF No. 60510	(US)/RAF	Bf109	**Z3267**	XR-D	1.0	C
19.08.41	P/O Morris W. **Fessler**	RAF No. 88385	(US)/RAF	Bf109	**Z3829**		1.0	P

Total: 12.5

Two future Eagle aces who started their career with 71 Sqn. Left: 'Wild Bill' Dunn from Minnesota. Not an original member, he joined 71 in May 1941. When war broke out, he immediately went to Canada to join the RCAF. He was told the RCAF was not accepting American citizens so switched to the Canadian Army and eventually joined the Seaforth Highlander's Regiment and, in December 1939, sailed for England. At the end of the Battle of Britain, the British needed pilots so the RAF tried to recruit Army and Navy personnel who had flying experience. During the summer of 1941, Dunn became one of the unit's most successful pilots until he was wounded in action on 27 August 1941, flying a Spitfire (see *SQUADRONS! 38*), the same day he achieved ace status. Recovered, he served with the RCAF until transferred to the USAAF in June 1943. Dunn survived the war.

Right: 'Pete' Peterson was from Idaho. Eager to fight in Europe, he sailed to the UK during the summer of 1940, at the height of the Battle of Britain, and joined the RAF in August. The USAAC training he had already received helped him speed up his training and he was soon posted to the newly formed 71 Sqn in November. In May 1941. he became a flight commander and, on 6 July, opened his score by claiming a probable Bf109. It was his only claim with the Hurricane as the squadron converted to the Spitfire soon after. In the following weeks, his tally increased, opening the way to a DFC awarded in October, and in November he was called to lead the squadron. He held this position until 71 was transferred to the USAAF as the 334th FS in September 1942. Just before his transfer, he was awarded the DSO and became the only 'Eagle' pilot to be so honoured. When he joined the USAAF, he had claimed six confirmed enemy aircraft destroyed, three more probables and six damaged. He continued the war by leading the 4th FG, the regrouping of the former Eagle squadrons, and adding two more confirmed victories to his credit. He survived the war and continued his career in the USAF before retiring as a major general in 1965.

Summary of the aircraft lost on Operations - 71 Squadron

Date	Pilot	S/N	Origin	Serial	Code	Fate
09.02.41	P/O Edwin E. **Orbison**	RAF No. 84659	(US)/RAF	**V6983***		†
15.02.41	P/O Vernon C. **Keough**	RAF No. 81620	(US)/RAF	**V7606***		†
26.04.41	P/O James L. **McGennis**	RAF No. 84658	(US)/RAF	**Z2494**		†
15.05.41	P/O John **Flynn**	RAF No. 61956	(US)/RAF	**Z2744**		-
17.05.41	P/O Stanley M. **Kolendorski**	RAF No. 84875	(US)/RAF	**Z3186**		†
02.07.41	P/O William I. **Hall**	RAF No. 61921	(US)/RAF	**Z3094**		PoW
19.08.41	P/O Virgil W. **Olson**	RAF No. 81619	(US)/RAF	**Z3494**		†

Total: 7

*Mk. I, the others Mk.II

Phil 'Zeke' Leckrone from Illinois in a Spitfire of 616 Sqn during the Battle of Britain. He was one of the seven American fighter pilots to fly during that period. Having gained a lot of flying experience in the USA, he managed to get a shortened course when he enlisted in the RAF in Canada in July 1940. He was posted to 616 Sqn in early September 1940. He reported to 71 Sqn three weeks later and was sadly killed in a flying accident on 5 January 1941.

Summary of the aircraft lost by accident - 71 Squadron

Date	Pilot	S/N	Origin	Serial	Code	Fate
01.01.41	P/O Vernon C. **Keough**	RAF No. 81620	(US)/RAF	**P3459***		-
05.01.41	P/O Philip H. **Leckrone**	RAF No. 84653	(US)/RAF	**V6636***		†
05.08.41	P/O William R. **Driver**	RAF No. 64869	(US)/RAF	**Z3266**		†

Total: 3

*Mk. I, the others Mk.II

Above: 71's members awaiting a scramble. From left to right: Luke E. Allen, Charles E. Bateman, Hilliard S. Fenlaw and Newton Anderson. Fenlaw, from Texas, was killed while serving with the squadron on 7 September 1941 (see *SQUADRONS! 25*). Bateman became a flight commander with 133 Sqn but suffered sinus problems that resulted in him being sent to Canada as an instructor. In September 1944, he transferred to the USAAF.
Below: Thomas P. McGerty from California under the nose of a Hurricane shortly after his arrival at the squadron in April 1941. He was killed in action on 17 September 1941 while above Bateman and Fenlow are posing on the left and the right wings respectively.

Taken from an unusual angle, an interesting view of F/L GA Brown's Hurricane Z3781/XR-A during the summer of 1941. Brown, a British officer, was the A Flight CO at the time.

No. 121 Squadron (code AV)

The second American-manned squadron, 121, was formed at Kirton in Lindsey on 14 May 1941. As with 71, the CO and the flight commanders were initially British, S/L R.P.R. Powell, Flight Lieutenants H.C .Kennard (A Flight) and R.C. Wilkinson (B Flight and formerly of 71 Squadron) respectively. American pilots began to be posted in from various fighter squadrons, including 71. The first ten Hurricanes, all Mk.Is, were taken on charge on the 17th but only six were serviceable; it would not be until mid-June that 121 would get its full complement of pilots and aircraft. Training soon began, but, in June, things went wrong for several of the pilots. On the 15th, P/O R.F. Patterson suffered an engine failure and was obliged to abandon the Hurricane over Old Leake, 3 miles north-east of Boston. One week later, P/O L.L. Laughlin was killed when his aircraft dove into the ground north-west of Scampton. The cause of the accident was never discovered. In July, as more pilots continued to arrive, training continued, mainly on Hurricane Mk.IIs which were not only more powerful but also in better shape, being brand new. Two Mk.IIs were soon lost in a mid-air collision over Lincoln on the 27th. Pilot Officer W.V. Shenk and Sgt B. Smith both managed to bale out safely.

The squadron became operational at the end of July and on 2 August the first sorties were carried out; six scrambles were flown throughout the day. The Luftwaffe was very active over the area on the 8th and 121 was obliged to maintain a high level of activity with various convoy patrols and scrambles performed that day. While 15 miles north-east of Hull, P/O S.R. Edner and Sgt J.J. Mooney sighted a Ju88 and immediately gave chase. They closed in and both opened fire on the Junkers until their ammunition gave out. The Ju88 was seen to lose height during the combat from 2,500 feet to 300 feet. No one could ascertain its eventual fate, but it was credited as being probably destroyed and shared by the two pilots. One week after becoming operational, 121 had already opened its scoreboard. Another line was added ten days later when the CO claimed a Bf109 as probably destroyed 7 miles south of Gravelines during a fighter sweep with the wing over the Continent (involving twelve Spitfires from 121). It was the first sweep carried out by the unit. Three more sweeps were flown before the end of the month, but otherwise 121 remained busy with less challenging (and less dangerous) patrols for a grand total of about 175 sorties flown in August. The number of sorties was cut by half in September, but the squadron recorded a death on the 15th when P/O E.W. Mason was killed while practicing aerobatics. At the end of September, 121 moved to Digby for a few days but was soon back at Kirton in Lindsey. On 2 October, F/Sgt R.F. Tilley took off in the evening for a dusk patrol but got lost soon after; owing to an R/T failure, he decided to bale out near Burton. While he managed to get out of his Hurricane, his landing did not go well and he fractured a leg. The rest of the month was rather uneventful except that, halfway through, the first Spitfire Mk.IIs were taken on charge. Operational flying ceased and conversion began, 121 eventually becoming operational on the Spitfire at the end of the month (see *SQUADRONS 38!*). The last Hurricanes were flown out in November.

Date	Pilot	S/N	Origin	Serial	Code	Fate
02.10.41	F/Sgt Reade F. **Tilley**	Can./ R.64276	(us)/RCAF	**Z5058**	AV-E	-

Total: 1

Reade F. Tilley from Florida in front of his Hurricane AV-F named 'Smocky Joe' (probably Z3669). Frustrated by the British climate, and seeking more action, he chose to serve overseas and fought brilliantly with 126 Sqn over Malta during 1942. He returned to the UK in August 1942 with seven confirmed victories and a DFC. Two months later, he transferred to the USAAF but did not fly on operations again.

Date	Pilot	S/N	Origin	Serial	Code	Fate
15.06.41	P/O Richard F. **PATTERSON**	Can./ J.2928	(us)/RCAF	**V7604***		-
21.06.41	P/O Loran L. **LAUGHLIN**	RAF No. 61925	(us)/RAF	**P3097***		†
27.07.41	P/O Warren V. **SHENK**	Can./ J.15072	(us)/RCAF	**Z3317**		-
	Sgt Bradley **SMITH**	Can./ R.67550	(us)/RCAF	**Z3422**		-
15.09.41	P/O Earl W. **MASON**	Can./J.15009	(us)/RCAF	**Z3667**		†

Total: 5

Mk. I, the others Mk.II

Richard F. Patterson from Virginia, in Hurricane Z3171/AV-B, wrecked the first 121 Sqn aircraft. Later on, in December 1941, he would also be the first of 121's pilots to be killed in action (see *SQUADRONS! 25*). Known serial/individual letters at that time were Z3076/J, Z3239/X, Z3399/C, Z3401/T, Z3427/R, Z3593/F, Z3596/J, Z3643/V, Z3653/Z, Z3666/J, Z3669/D, Z3670/G, Z3770/S, Z5048/E, Z5058/E, Z5137/L, Z5670/G and AP521/AV-M.

Founding members with interesting careers:

Top left: P/O C.W. McColpin from New York poses for the photographer after having been awarded the DFC with 71 Sqn. He was one of the few American pilots to have served in all three Eagle squadrons and reached ace status with 71 after he joined the unit in September 1941. In 1942, while at the head of 133 Sqn, he transferred to the USAAF as CO of the 336th FS and retired as a major general 26 years later.

Top right: P/O J.A. Campbell from California. Joining early in June, he remained with the squadron until October 1941 when he was posted to 258 Sqn after having asked to serve overseas so he could see more action. His new unit eventually arrived, via the Middle East and HMS *Indomitable*, in Singapore at the height of the fighting at the end of January 1942. The combat was desperate and he was shot down on 28 February 1942; by this time he was flying with 605 Sqn and close to becoming an ace. He managed to evade for a few weeks but was eventually captured on 20 March, the only Eagle pilot captured by the Japanese. He was released in September 1945; a DFC had been gazetted in August 1942 for his actions in the Far East.

Bottom left: P/O S.R. Edner from Minnesota. He became the squadron's only ace and one of the few to receive the DFC. He also transferred to the USAAF in September 1942 and eventually became a PoW on 8 March 1944. He remained with the USAAF/USAF but was executed as a member of the American Military Assistance and Advisory Group during the Greek Civil War in January 1949.

<u>**No. 133 Squadron (code MD)**</u>

The continuous flow of Americans enlisting in either the RAF or RCAF saw the formation of a third fighter unit, No. 133 Squadron, just ten weeks after the formation of the second 'Eagle' Squadron, 121. Formed at Coltishall on 1 August 1941, training immediately began on Hurricane Mk.IIs under the guidance of a British CO, S/L G.A. Brown, formerly of 71 Squadron. He was backed initially by his two flight commanders, also British, Flight Lieutenants H.A.S. Johnstone and G.W. Scott, who joined later on. The squadron re-located to Duxford on 15 August. Scott stayed for a short time before being posted to 601 Squadron at the beginning of September; his position was taken over by an American, F/L A. Mamedoff, posted in from 71 Squadron. He was one of the very few experienced American pilots to serve with 133 as, during August, new arrivals were all fresh graduates from No. 56 Operational Training Unit. Training progressed without major incidents until 27 September when Pilot Officers W.G. Soares and C.S. Barell collided while turning on approach to land. Both crashed at Anton Hill and were killed. Two days later, 133 became operational and, during the day, two scrambles were flown, as was a sweep over the North Sea. The next day, the squadron again flew patrols and a North Sea sweep. On 3 October, 133 moved to Fowlmere before moving to Eglington, the unit's new permanent base, on the 8th. The ferry flight turned into a dramatic event as fifteen Hurricanes were caught by bad weather and four pilots were killed (Pilot Officers W.J. White, R.N. Stout Jr and H.H. McCall, and the new B Flight CO, F/L Mamedoff. Mamedoff was replaced by another 71 Squadron pilot, F/L C.E. Bateman, who arrived on the 23rd. The squadron was withdrawn from service for a couple of days to recover from these sad losses. Operational activity resumed on the 14th. It was not long before the squadron suffered another accidental loss. On 23 October, P/O G..R Bruce, a Canadian-born American, was returning from a convoy patrol when he made an unauthorised low pass over the airfield. Unfortunately, he struck a tree and crashed. Four days later, P/O J.G. Coxetter was killed when, during a navex, it is believed he entered cloud and lost control of his aircraft. He chose to abandon the Hurricane but did so too low; his chute did not have time to open properly. It was a sad month, even though the arrival of Spitfire IIs suggested a promising future. In November, 133 flew both types even though the Hurricanes began to be progressively withdrawn. December saw the last Hurricane sorties with a convoy patrol by Pilot Officers E. Doorly and C.A. Cook. With a new commander, S/L E.H. Thomas, who had taken over on 27 November, the squadron was ready to make another start. About 100 sorties were flown on Hurricanes by 133 Squadron (see *SQUADRONS! 38* and *25* for the unit's operational use of the Spitfire Mk.II and Mk.V).

George Brown (left) joined the RAF on a short service commission in April 1937. At the outbreak of the war, he was serving with 66 Sqn with which he would make his two claims, one confirmed Ju87 and another unconfirmed over Rotterdam on 13 May. Soon after, he was posted to 253 Sqn and participated in the Battle of Britain until being wounded in action on 30 August. He recovered from his injuries and was posted to the newly formed 71 Sqn as a flight commander. He remained with 71 until August 1941 when he was chosen to lead the third and last Eagle squadron, 133, then under formation, and bring the new pilots up to operational standard. He left the unit in November for a staff appointment at HQ Fighter Command and was awarded the DFC the following month. For his second tour of operations, he was given command of 257 Sqn, flying Typhoons, and led the unit until the end of his tour in April 1943. No more operational postings followed, but he served in the Middle East until the end of war.

Squadron Leader E.H. Thomas (right) arrived at the very end of the 133's Hurricane era. This Battle of Britain veteran had previously led 611 Sqn before being posted to 133 in November 1941. He left 133 Sqn in August 1942 to become wing leader of the Biggin Hill and, later, Hornchurch Wings until November. Because of health problems, he had to relinquish his commission in September 1944, but with a DSO and DFC and Bar to his name.

Date	Pilot	S/N	Origin	Serial	Code	Fate
23.10.41	P/O George R. **Bruce**	RAF No. 67580	(US)/RAF	**Z3649**		†
			Total: 1			

Summary of the aircraft lost by accident - 133 Squadron

Date	Pilot	S/N	Origin	Serial	Code	Fate
27.09.41	P/O Walter G. **Soares**	RAF No. 100532	(US)/RAF	**Z3335**	MD-B	†
	P/O Charles S. **Barrell**	RAF No. 102519	(US)/RAF	**Z3828**	MD-F	†
08.10.41	F/L Andrew B. **Mamedoff**	RAF No. 81621	(US)/RAF	**Z3781**	MD-U	†
	P/O William J. **White**	RAF No. 100535	(US)/RAF	**Z3457**	MD-Y	†
	P/O Roy N. **Stout** Jr.	RAF No. 100531	(US)/RAF	**Z3253**		†
	P/O Hugh H. **McCall**	RAF No.67583	(US)/RAF	**Z3677**		†
27.10.41	P/O James G. **Coxetter**	RAF No.104392	(US)/RAF	**Z3182**		†
			Total: 7			

Among the first pilots to be posted to the newly formed 133 Sqn, P/O H.H. Strickland (left) from Louisiana was peculiar as he was 38 when he joined the squadron, one of the oldest Eagle pilots to fly for the RAF. However, he had flying experience of over 2,000 hours when he enlisted. He didn't stay long with 133, being posted to 71 a few weeks later to reinforce that unit after it experienced heavy losses. He eventually transferred to the USAAF in September 1942 and survived the war. Posted in at the same time as Strickland, James C. Nelson, from Colorado, served with 133 between September 1941 and September 1942 when the unit became the 336th FS of the USAAF. He elected not to transfer to the USAAF and continued to serve in the RAF and eventually assumed command of 124 Sqn in December that year. When he left 124 in June 1943, he went on to serve as a test pilot, but was involved in a serious accident on 23 August 1944 while flying a Mosquito XVI. He never fully recovered and was eventually medically discharged in April 1945.

✝

IN MEMORIAM

Hurricane Mk I & Mk II - The Eagle Squadrons

Name	Service No	Rank	Age	Origin	Date	Serial
BARRELL, Charles Sewall	RAF No. 102519	P/O	29	(US)/RAF	27.09.41	Z3828
BRUCE, George Russell	RAF No. 67580	P/O	27	(US)/RAF	23.10.41	Z3649
COXETTER, James Geiger	RAF No. 104392	P/O	23	(US)/RAF	27.10.41	Z3182
DRIVER, William Richard	RAF No. 64869	P/O	22	(US)/RAF	05.08.41	Z3266
KEOUGH, Vernon Charles	RAF No. 81620	P/O	29	(US)/RAF	15.02.41	V7606
KOLENDORSKI, Stanley Michel	RAF No. 84875	F/O	25	(US)/RAF	17.05.41	Z3186
LAUGHLIN, Loran Lee	RAF No. 61925	P/O	29	(US)/RAF	21.06.41	P3097
LECKRONE, Philip Howard	RAF No. 84653	P/O	28	(US)/RAF	05.01.41	V6636
MAMEDOFF, Andrew B.	RAF No. 81621	F/L	30	(US)/RAF	08.10.41	Z3781
MASON, Earl Wallace	CAN./ J.15009	P/O	24	(US)/RCAF	15.09.41	Z3667
McCALL, Hugh Harrison	RAF No. 67583	P/O	24	(US)/RAF	08.10.41	Z3677
McGINNIS, James Leland	RAF No. 84658	P/O	29	(US)/RAF	26.04.41	Z2494
OLSON, Virgin Willis	RAF No. 81619	P/O	28	(US)/RAF	19.08.41	Z3494
ORBISON, Edwin Ezell	RAF No. 84659	P/O	23	(US)/RAF	09.02.41	V6983
SOARES, Walter Gordon	RAF No. 100532	P/O	22	(US)/RAF	27.09.41	Z3335
STOUT, Roy Neal Jr.	RAF No. 100531	P/O	24	(US)/RAF	08.10.41	Z3253
WHITE, William Joseph	RAF No. 100535	P/O	21	(US)/RAF	08.10.41	Z3457

Total: 17

USA: 17

Hawker Hurricane Mk I V7608
No. 71 (Eagle) Squadron
Kirton-in-Lindsey (UK), winter 1940-1941

Hawker Hurricane Mk I Vxxx7
No. 71 (Eagle) Squadron
Martlesham Heath (UK), spring 1941

Hawker Hurricane Mk.IIB Z3781
No. 71 (Eagle) Squadron
Flight Lieutenant George A. BROWN (RAF)
North Weald (UK), summer 1941

Hawker Hurricane Mk.IIB Z3267
No. 71 (Eagle) Squadron
Pilot Officer William R. DUNN (USA)
North Weald (UK), summer 1941

Hawker Hurricane Mk.IIB Z3427
No. 121 (Eagle) Squadron
Kirton-in-Lindsey (UK), August 1941

Donald James Matthew BLAKESLEE DFC

Supermarine Spitfire Mk.VB EN951
No. 133 (Eagle) Squadron
Flight Lieutenant D. J. M. Blakeslee
CAN./ J.4351
Gravesend (UK), August 1942

Charles Cuthbertson LEARMONTH DFC*

Douglas Boston Mk. III A28-9 (ex-AL891)
No. 22 Squadron RAAF
Squadron Leader C. C. Learmonth
Aus. 385
Port Moresby (New Guinea), spring 1943

Hans Anton MAURENBRECHER

Curtiss P-40N-35-CU C3-560
No. 120 (NEI) Squadron
Major H. Maurenbrecher
Biak (New Guinea), 1945-1946

Roland Prosper BEAMONT DSO* DFC*

Hawker Tempest Mk V JN751
No. 150 Wing
Wing Commander R. P. Beamont
RAF No. 41819
Bradwell Bay (UK), April 1944

Ronald Thomas SUSANS DSO DFC

North American P-51D-25-NT A68-724
No. 77 squadron, RAAF
Squadron Leader R. T. Susans
O4561
Bofu (Japan), 1947

James Henry LACEY DFM*

Supermarine Spitfire Mk XIV RN135
No. 17 Squadron
Squadron Leader J. H. Lacey
RAF No. 112709
Seletar (Singapore), autumn 1945

Introducing's RAF In Combat and Bravo Bravo Aviation's collection of
highly-detailed and historically accurate, high-quality aviation prints.
For more information on available prints, please visit :

or

Prints available for this book:

PL-040: G.A. Brown
PL-055: W.R. Dunn
PL-185: W.M. Churchill
PL-186: W.E.G. Taylor